Counting Numbers
1 to 5

Name
....
Date

To parents   Write your child's name and date in the boxes above. Teach your child the order of numbers from 1 to 5 by saying the numbers aloud with him or her at first.

■ Draw a line from ① to ⑤ in order while saying each number aloud.

| 1 | 2 | 3 | 4 | 5 |

1

W9-APH-261

■ Draw a line from ① to ⑤ in order while saying each number aloud.

| 1 | 2 | 3 | 4 | 5 |

■ Draw a line from ① to ⑩ in order while saying each number aloud.

| 1 | 2 | 3 | 4 | 5 | 6 | 7 | 8 | 9 | 10 |

■ Draw a line from ① to ⑩ in order while saying each number aloud.

1 2 3 4 5 6 7 8 9 10

Counting Numbers 1 to 15

Name

Date

■ Draw a line from ① to ⑮ in order while saying each number aloud.

| 1 | 2 | 3 | 4 | 5 | 6 | 7 | 8 | 9 | 10 | 11 | 12 | 13 | 14 | 15 |

Draw a line from ① to ⑮ in order while saying each number aloud.

1 2 3 4 5 6 7 8 9 10 11 12 13 14 15

6

Counting Numbers
1 to 20

Name

Date

■ Draw a line from ① to ⑳ in order while saying each number aloud.

| 1 | 2 | 3 | 4 | 5 | 6 | 7 | 8 | 9 | 10 | 11 | 12 | 13 | 14 | 15 | 16 | 17 | 18 | 19 | 20 |

■ Draw a line from ① to ⑳ in order while saying each number aloud.

| 1 | 2 | 3 | 4 | 5 | 6 | 7 | 8 | 9 | 10 | 11 | 12 | 13 | 14 | 15 | 16 | 17 | 18 | 19 | 20 |

Counting Numbers
1 to 25

Name

....

Date

To parents Your child's lines may not be steady at first, but they should improve with practice. Make sure to praise your child for his or her hard work.

■ Draw a line from ① to ㉕ in order while saying each number aloud.

| 1 | 2 | 3 | 4 | 5 | 6 | 7 | 8 | 9 | 10 | 11 | 12 | 13 | 14 | 15 | 16 | 17 | 18 | 19 | 20 | 21 | 22 | 23 | 24 | 25 |

■ Draw a line from ① to ㉕ in order while saying each number aloud.

| 1 | 2 | 3 | 4 | 5 | 6 | 7 | 8 | 9 | 10 | 11 | 12 | 13 | 14 | 15 | 16 | 17 | 18 | 19 | 20 | 21 | 22 | 23 | 24 | 25 |

Counting Numbers
1 to 30

Name

....

Date

■ Draw a line from ① to ㉚ in order while saying each number aloud.

| 1 | 2 | 3 | 4 | 5 | 6 | 7 | 8 | 9 | 10 | 11 | 12 | 13 | 14 | 15 | 16 | 17 | 18 | 19 | 20 | 21 | 22 | 23 | 24 | 25 | 26 | 27 | 28 | 29 | 30 |

Draw a line from ① to ㉚ in order while saying each number aloud.

| 1 | 2 | 3 | 4 | 5 | 6 | 7 | 8 | 9 | 10 | 11 | 12 | 13 | 14 | 15 | 16 | 17 | 18 | 19 | 20 | 21 | 22 | 23 | 24 | 25 | 26 | 27 | 28 | 29 | 30 |

Counting Numbers
1 to 10

Name

Date

To parents For additional fun, ask your child to guess what is in the picture before he or she connects the dots. Once your child is done, they can also color in the object they have created!

■ Draw a line from 1 to 10 in order while saying each number aloud.

| 1 | 2 | 3 | 4 | 5 | 6 | 7 | 8 | 9 | 10 |

13

(tree)

1 to 15

■ Draw a line from 1 to 15 in order while saying each number aloud.

| 1 | 2 | 3 | 4 | 5 | 6 | 7 | 8 | 9 | 10 | 11 | 12 | 13 | 14 | 15 |

(ship)

Counting Numbers
1 to 20

Name

....

Date

To parents   Remember to encourage your child as the exercises get more challenging. If your child has difficulty finding the next number, please point it out for him or her. The object is to practice counting numbers and to enjoy the process.

■ Draw a line from 1 to 20 in order while saying each number aloud.

1	2	3	4	5	6	7	8	9	10	11	12	13	14	15	16	17	18	19	20

(slide)

1 to 25

■ Draw a line from 1 to 25 in order while saying each number aloud.

| 1 | 2 | 3 | 4 | 5 | 6 | 7 | 8 | 9 | 10 | 11 | 12 | 13 | 14 | 15 | 16 | 17 | 18 | 19 | 20 | 21 | 22 | 23 | 24 | 25 |

(hippo)

Counting Numbers
1 to 30

Name

Date

To parents   If these exercises are becoming too difficult for your child, try *My Book of NUMBERS 1-30* or *My Book of NUMBER GAMES 1-70* for more practice.

■ Draw a line from 1 to 30 in order while saying each number aloud.

1	2	3	4	5	6	7	8	9	10	11	12	13	14	15	16	17	18	19	20	21	22	23	24	25	26	27	28	29	30

(giraffe)

1 to 30

■ Draw a line from 1 to 30 in order while saying each number aloud.

| 1 | 2 | 3 | 4 | 5 | 6 | 7 | 8 | 9 | 10 | 11 | 12 | 13 | 14 | 15 | 16 | 17 | 18 | 19 | 20 | 21 | 22 | 23 | 24 | 25 | 26 | 27 | 28 | 29 | 30 |

(crocodile)

Writing Numbers
1 and **2**

Name

Date

To parents   Now your child will practice tracing the numbers one through ten. Though the stroke path on this page is wide, it may be challenging for your child to draw straight lines. It is more important that your child enjoy learning than it is for him or her to correctly write these numbers. Praise your child's efforts no matter the results.

■ Write the number 1 and say it aloud.

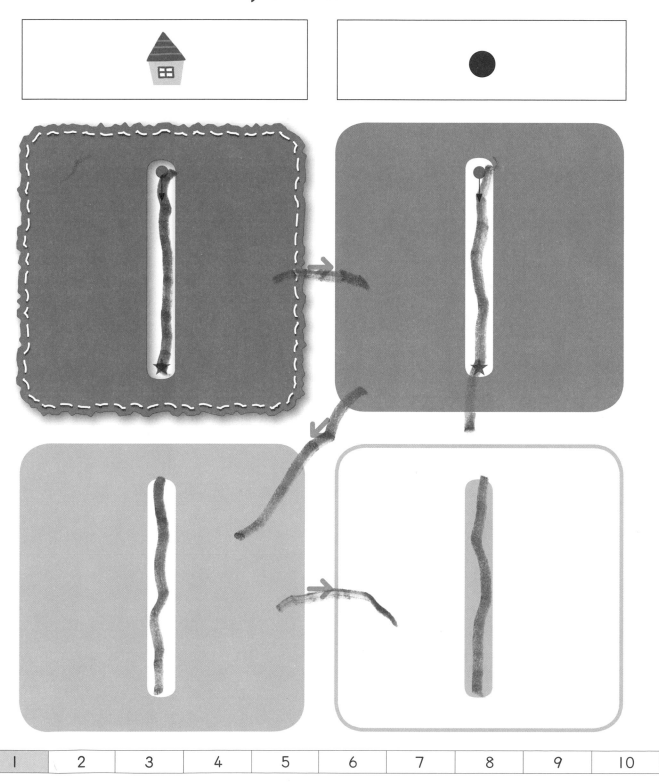

1	2	3	4	5	6	7	8	9	10

■ Write the number 2 and say it aloud.

I	2	3	4	5	6	7	8	9	10

Writing Numbers
3 and **4**

Name

Date

■ Write the number 3 and say it aloud.

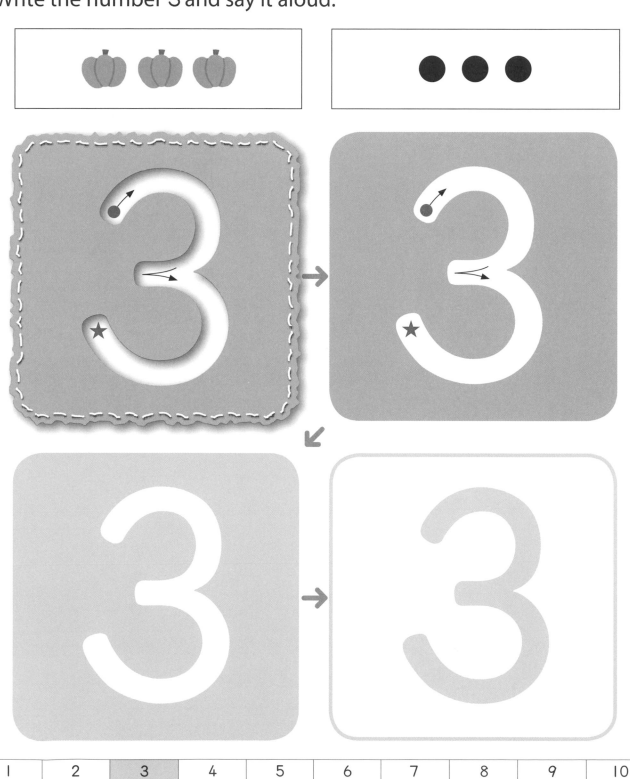

I	2	3	4	5	6	7	8	9	10

Write the number 4 and say it aloud.

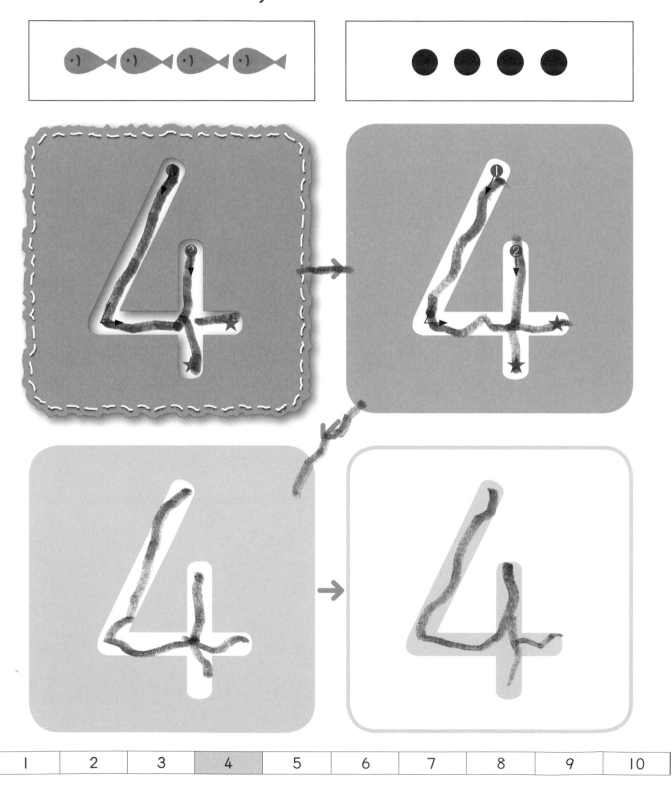

| 1 | 2 | 3 | 4 | 5 | 6 | 7 | 8 | 9 | 10 |

Writing Numbers
5 and 6

Name

Date

To parents Five is a difficult number to write. Try helping your child trace the first example, or try pointing out the stroke order, so that your child has a little help the first time he or she attempts to write the number.

■ Write the number 5 and say it aloud.

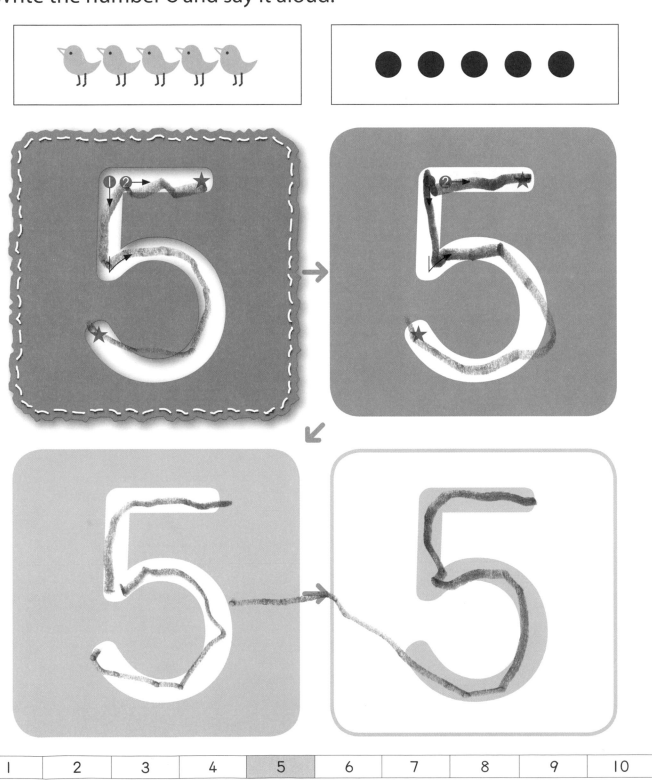

| I | 2 | 3 | 4 | 5 | 6 | 7 | 8 | 9 | 10 |

■ Write the number 6 and say it aloud.

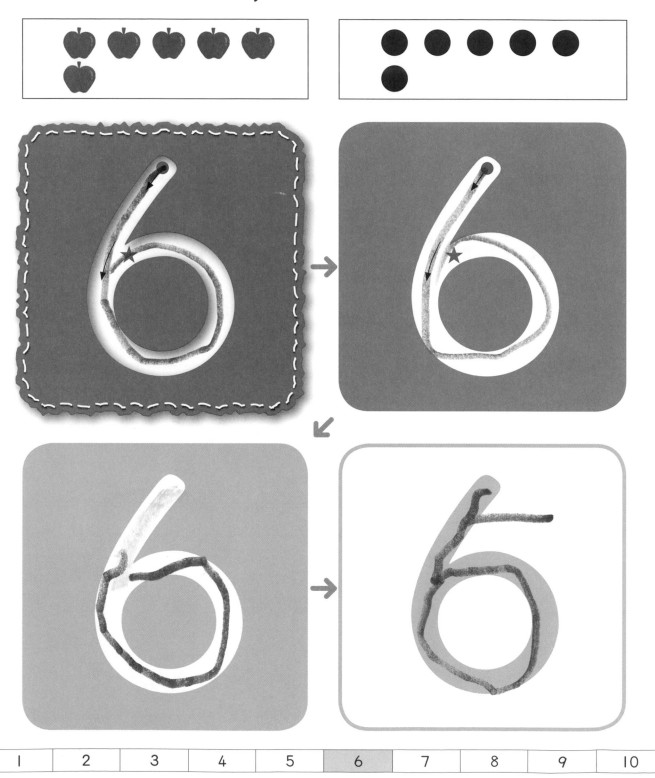

| 1 | 2 | 3 | 4 | 5 | 6 | 7 | 8 | 9 | 10 |

Writing Numbers
7 and 8

■ Write the number 7 and say it aloud.

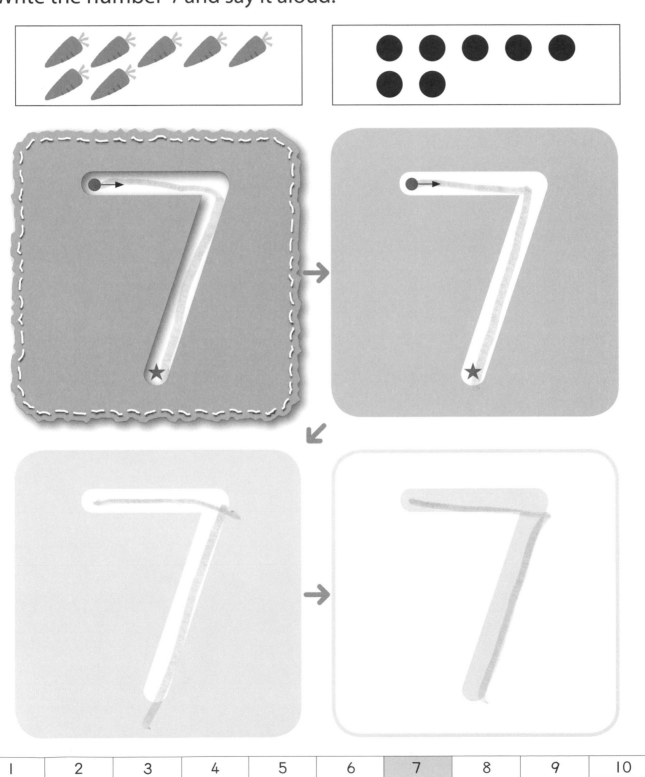

| 1 | 2 | 3 | 4 | 5 | 6 | 7 | 8 | 9 | 10 |

25

■ Write the number 8 and say it aloud.

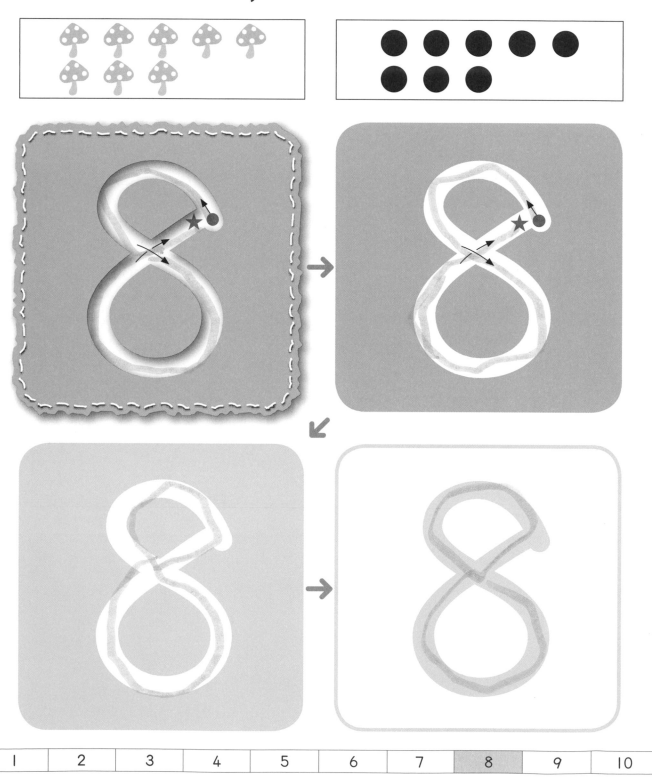

| 1 | 2 | 3 | 4 | 5 | 6 | 7 | 8 | 9 | 10 |

Writing Numbers
9 and 10

Name ....

Date ....

To parents Try helping your child practice counting on a daily basis. Find opportunities to have fun with numbers at the grocery store, in the park, or wherever you are.

■ Write the number 9 and say it aloud.

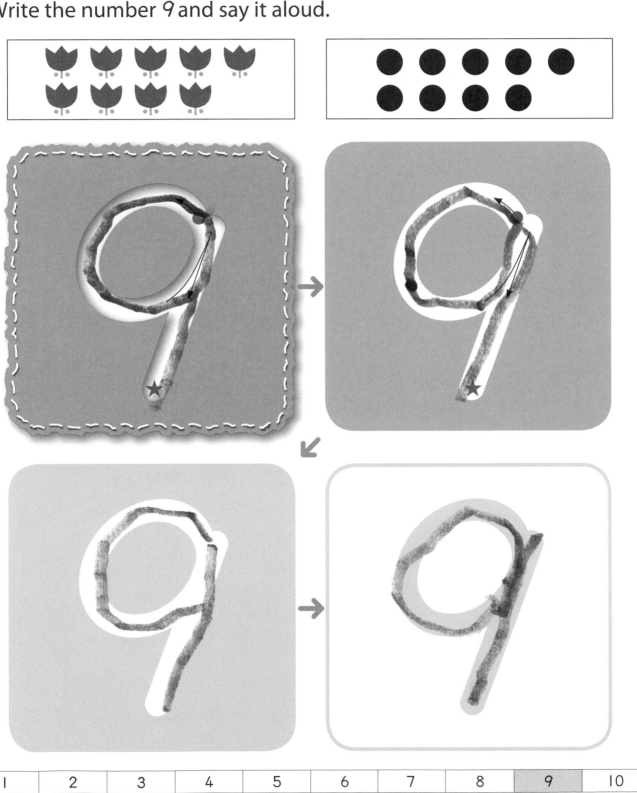

1	2	3	4	5	6	7	8	9	10

■ Write the number 10 and say it aloud.

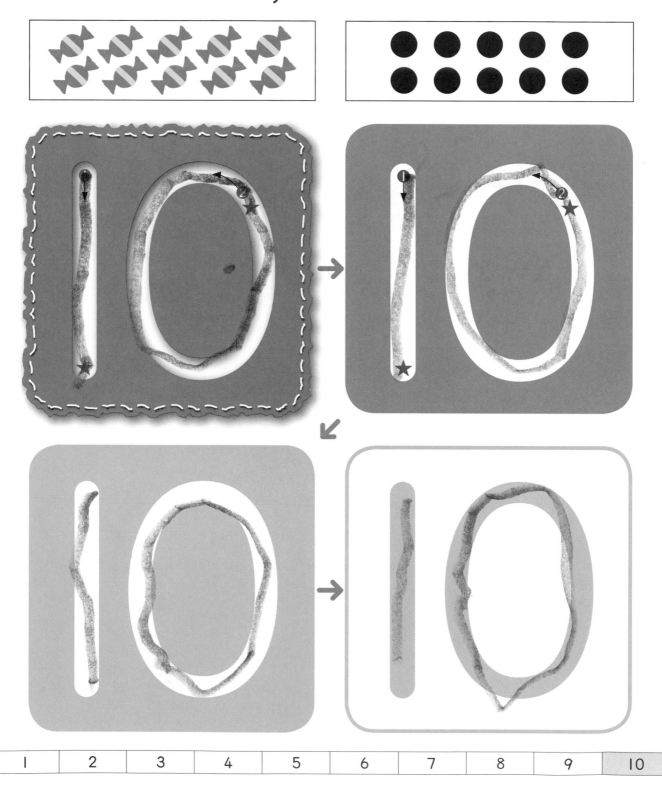

| 1 | 2 | 3 | 4 | 5 | 6 | 7 | 8 | 9 | 10 |

To parents Now that there is no stroke order shown, and the space is narrower, your child may encounter some difficulty. If your child struggles to write in the provided space, try *My Book of NUMBERS 1-30* for more practice.

■ How many are there? Trace the numbers and fill the empty boxes.

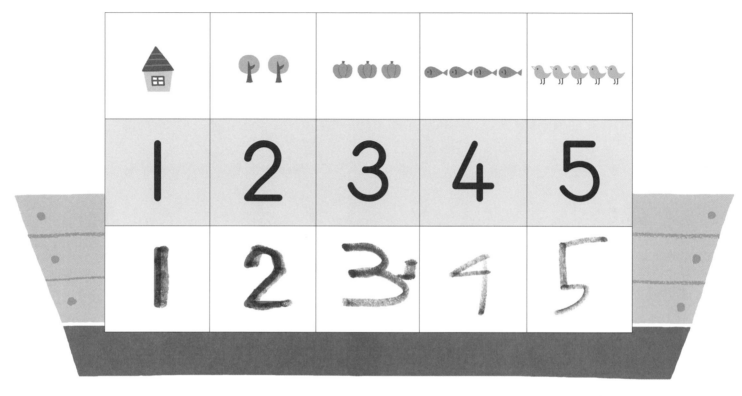

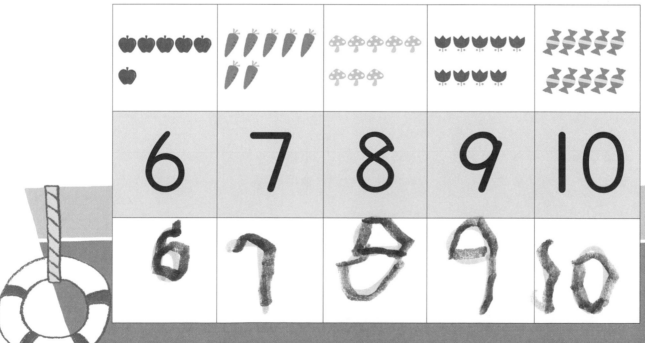

■ How many are there? Trace the numbers and fill the empty boxes.

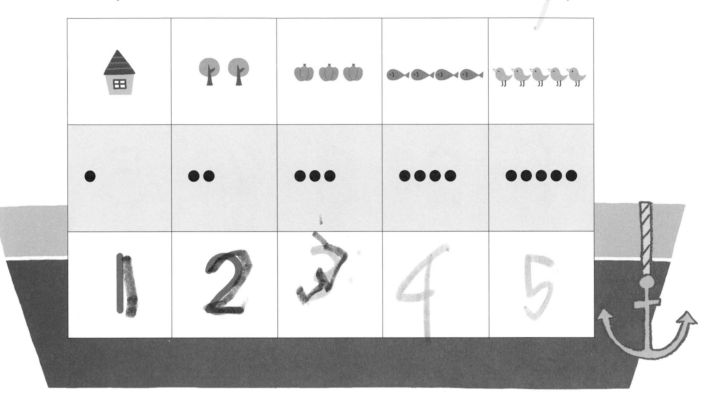

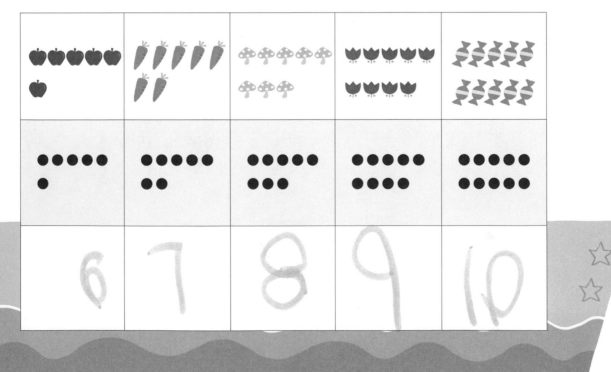

■ How many are there? Trace and write the numbers.

•	••	•••	••••	•••••
1	2	3	4	5
••••• •	••••• ••	••••• •••	••••• ••••	••••• •••••
6	7	8	9	10
••••• ••••• •	••••• ••••• ••	••••• ••••• •••	••••• ••••• ••••	••••• ••••• •••••
11	12	13	14	15

31

■ Trace the numbers. Then fill in the missing numbers. Say each number aloud.

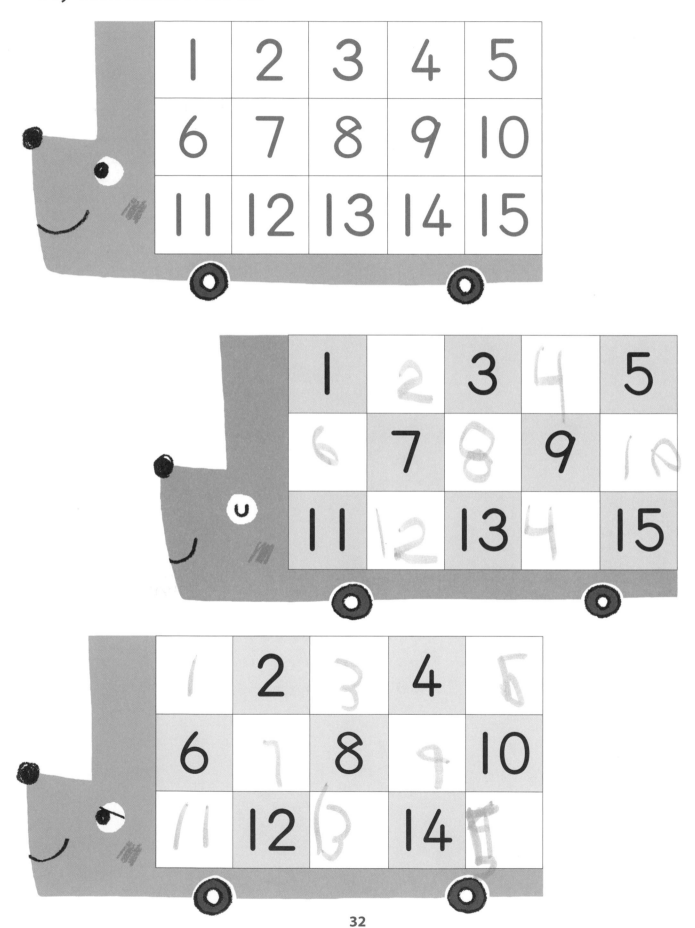

How Many?
1 to 20

Name

Date

■ How many are there? Trace and write the numbers.

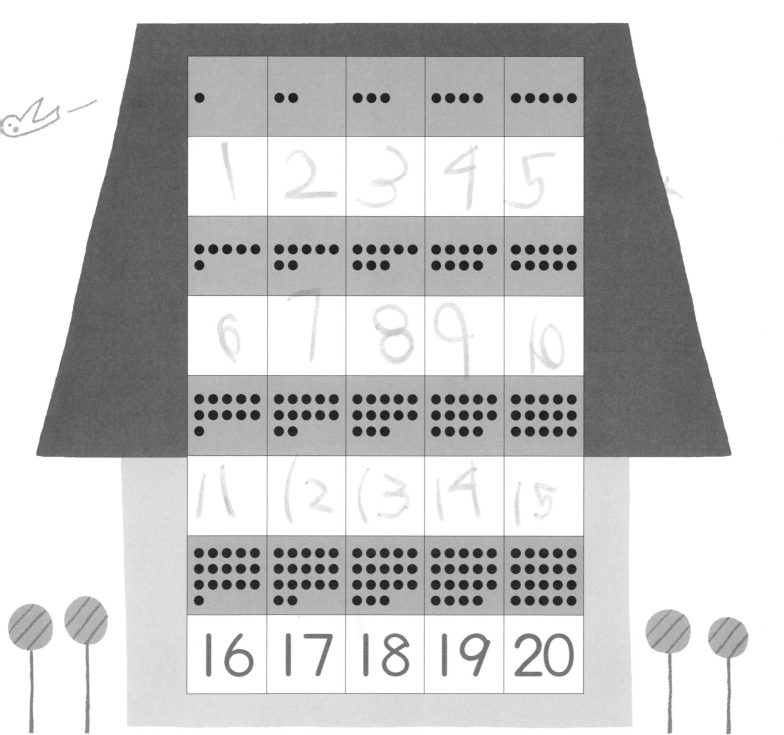

■ Trace the numbers. Then fill in the missing numbers.
Say each number aloud.

1	2	3	4	5
6	7	8	9	10
11	12	13	14	15
16	17	18	19	20

1		3		5
	7		9	
11		13		15
	17		19	

How Many?
1 to 25

Name

Date

■ How many are there? Trace and write the numbers.

21 22 23 24 25

35

■ Trace the numbers. Then fill in the missing numbers.
Say each number aloud.

1	2	3	4	5
6	7	8	9	10
11	12	13	14	15
16	17	18	19	20
21	22	23	24	25

	2		4	
6		8		10
	12		14	
16		18		20
	22		24	

How Many?
1 to 30

Name

Date

To parents The numbers up to 30 are considered the kindergarten standard in most places. If your child is able to complete these pages, he or she is more than ready for kindergarten. More probably, your child has benefitted from the practice and will be prepared to see similar exercises when he or she attends the first day at kindergarten.

■ How many are there? Trace and write the numbers.

| 26 | 27 | 28 | 29 | 30 |

■ Trace the numbers. Then fill in the missing numbers.
  Say each number aloud.

1	2	3	4	5
6	7	8	9	10
11	12	13	14	15
16	17	18	19	20
21	22	23	24	25
26	27	28	29	30

1		3		5
	7		9	
11		13		15
	17		19	
21		23		25
	27		29	

38

Counting Numbers
1 to 30

■ Fill in the missing numbers. Say each number aloud.

	2		4	
6		8		10
	12		14	
16		18		20
	22		24	
26		28		30

1				
6	7	8	9	10
16	17	18	19	20
26	27	28	29	30

■ Fill in the missing numbers. Say each number aloud.

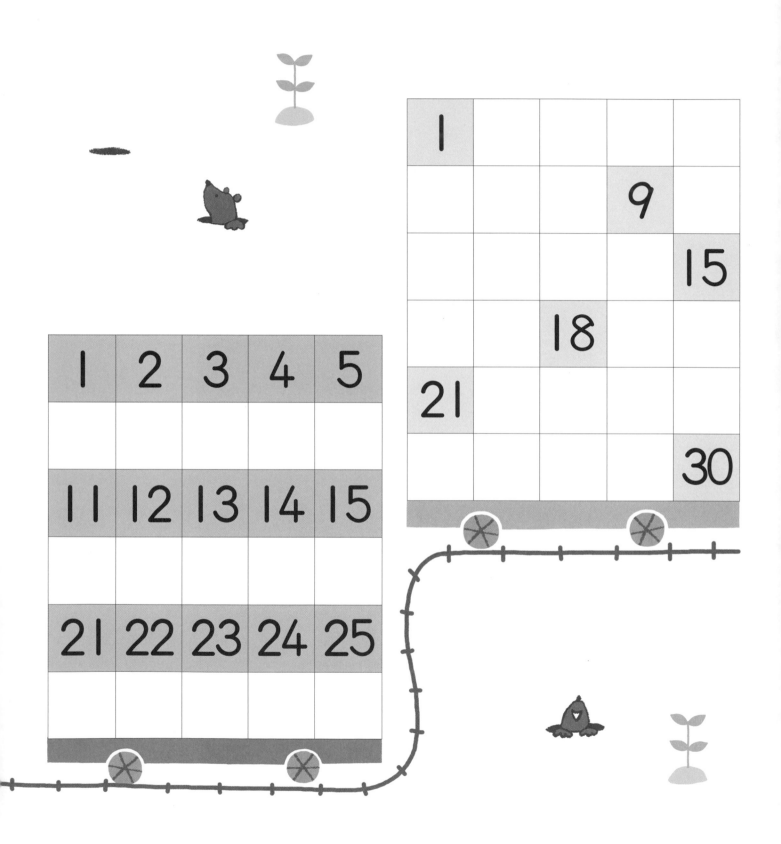

Grid 1 (left):

1	2	3	4	5
11	12	13	14	15
21	22	23	24	25

Grid 2 (right):

1				
			9	
				15
		18		
21				
				30

To parents The following pages will give your child the chance to refine his or her motor control skills while learning the names of common shapes. Try pointing out shapes in the world around your child, as this will help him or her remember their names.

■ Draw the shapes below.

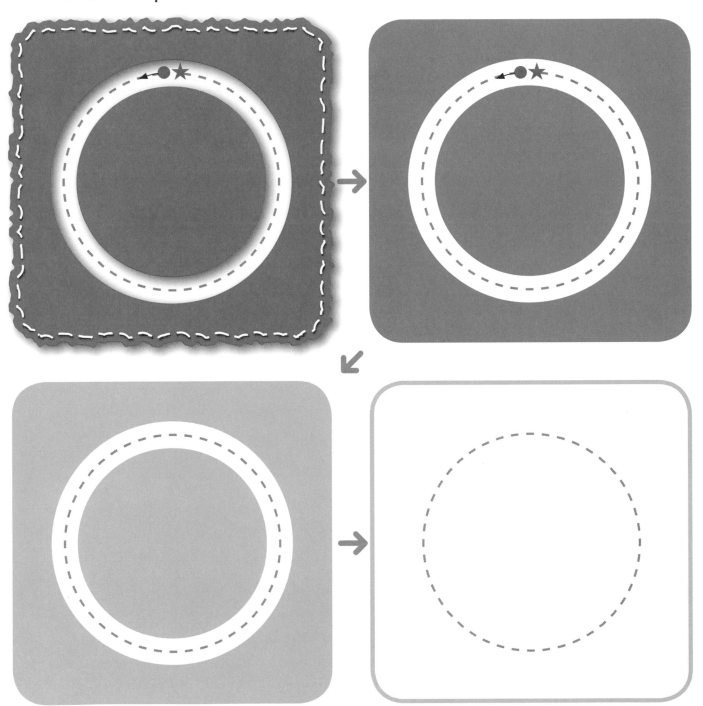

Oval

■ Draw the shapes below.

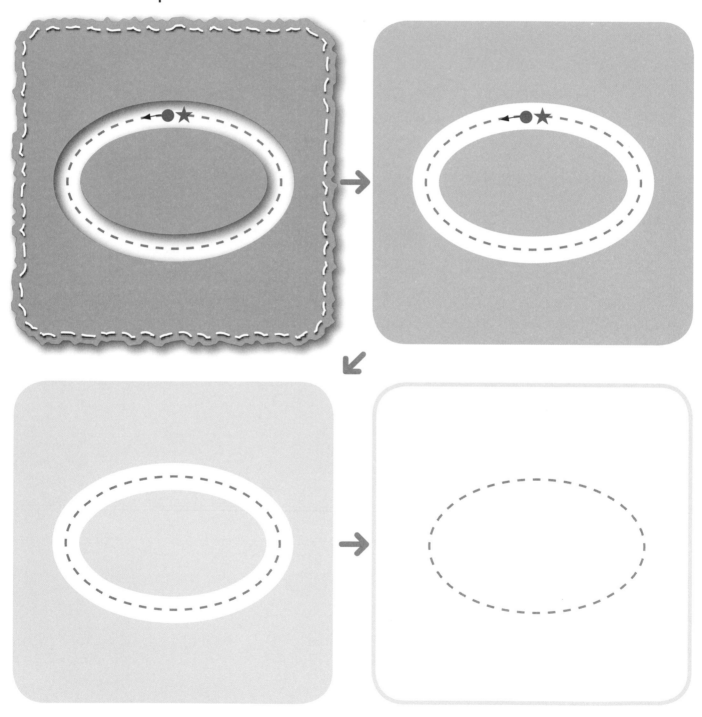

To parents In order to help your child understand what makes a square, you could point out the characteristics of the shape. Show your child that a square has four equal, straight sides, for example.

■ Draw the shapes below.

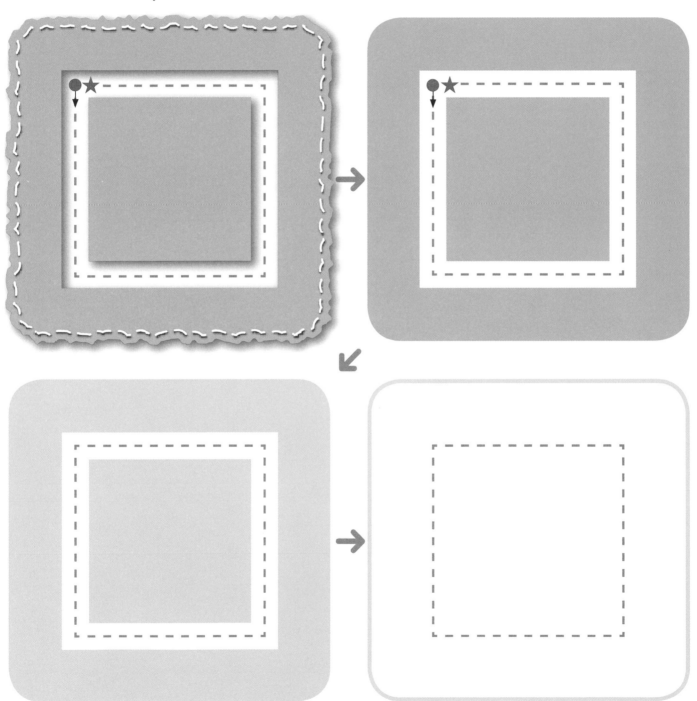

Rectangle

■ Draw the shapes below.

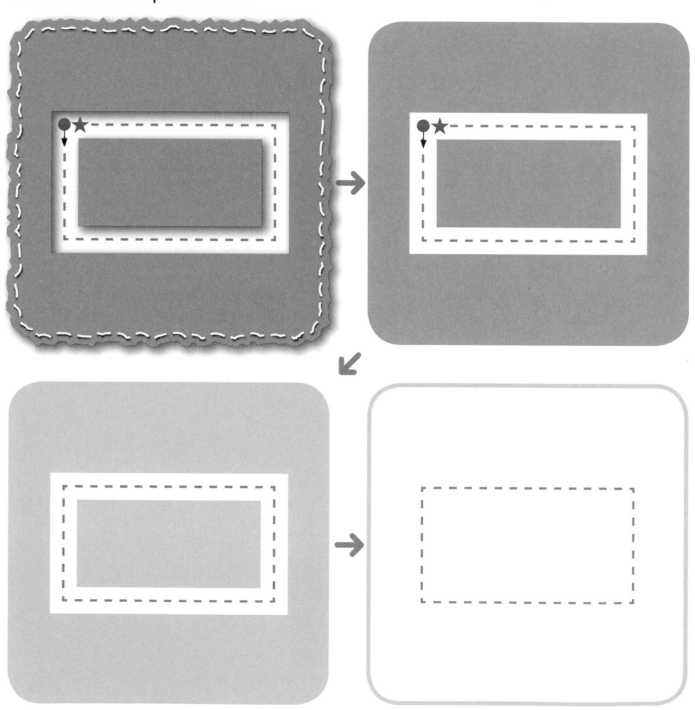

■ Draw the shapes below.

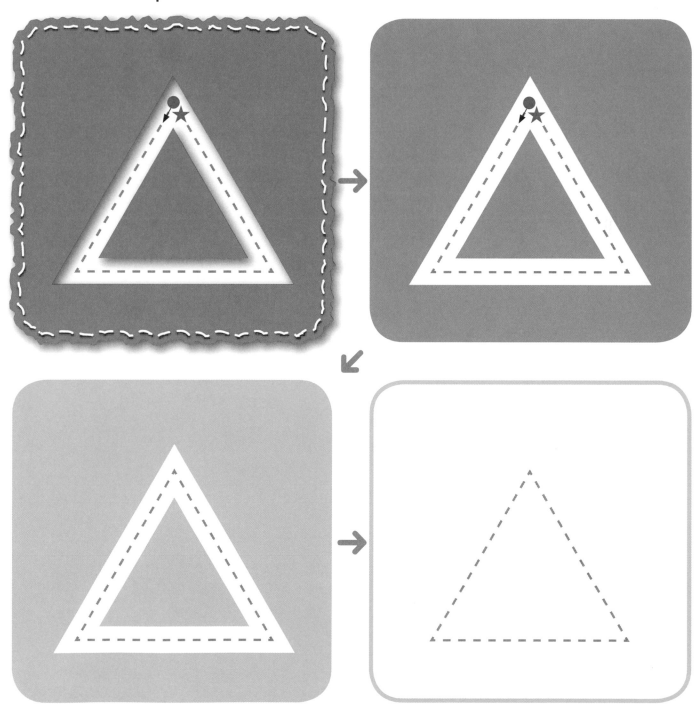

Diamond（Rhombus）

■ Draw the shapes below.

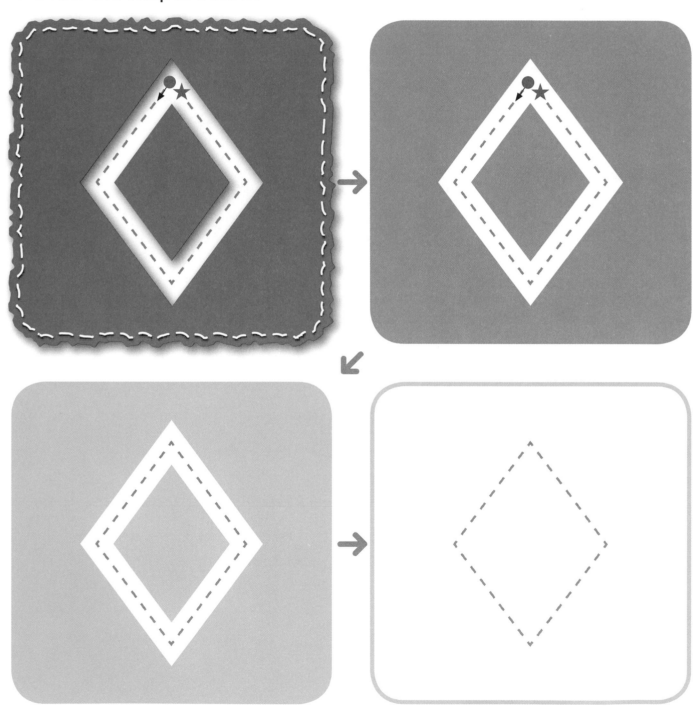

What is the Same Shape?

Name
....

Date

To parents This page will help your child spot similarities in shapes of different sizes. If your child struggles to find the correct shape, try pointing out the characteristics of the shape you are looking for. For example, a circle is perfectly round – what other shapes on this page are perfectly round?

■ Circle the shapes below that are the same shape as the sample.

sample

circle

■ Circle the shapes below that are the same shape as the sample.

sample

square

What is the Same Shape?

Name

....

Date

■ Circle the shapes below that are the same shape as the sample.

49

■ Circle the shapes below that are the same shape as the samples.

sample	sample	sample
oval	rectangle	diamond

What is the Same Shape and Color?

Name

Date

■ Circle the shape below that is the same shape and color as the sample.

51

■ Circle the shapes below that are the same shape and color as the samples.

sample	sample
[blue square]	[yellow triangle]
blue square	yellow triangle

What is the Same Shape and Color?

Name

Date

■ Circle the shapes below that are the same shape and color as the samples.

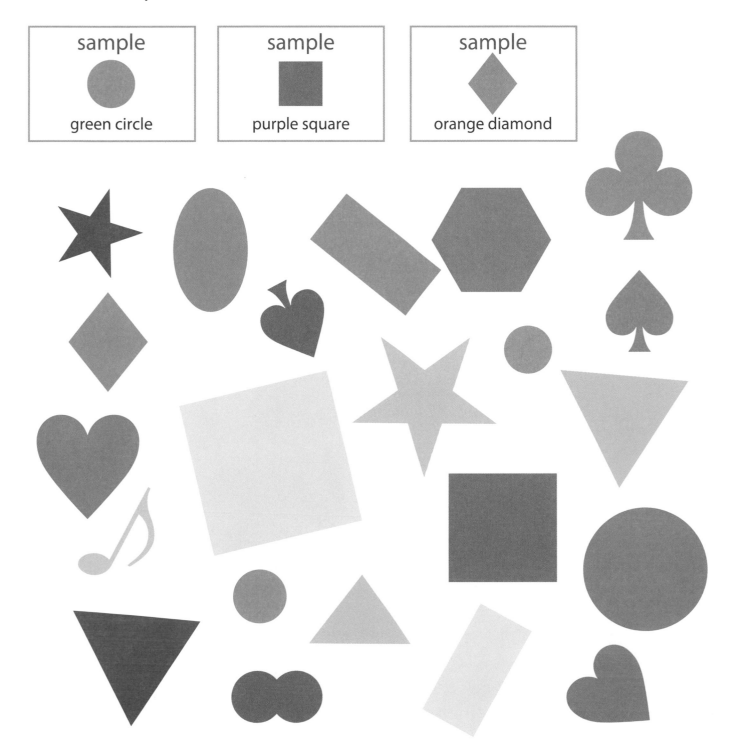

sample

green circle

sample

purple square

sample

orange diamond

■ Circle the shapes below that are the same shape and color as the samples.

sample	sample	sample
blue circle	yellow square	red triangle

What is the Same Shape and Color?

Name

Date

■ Find the shapes shown in the samples below.
  Then color them the same color as the sample.

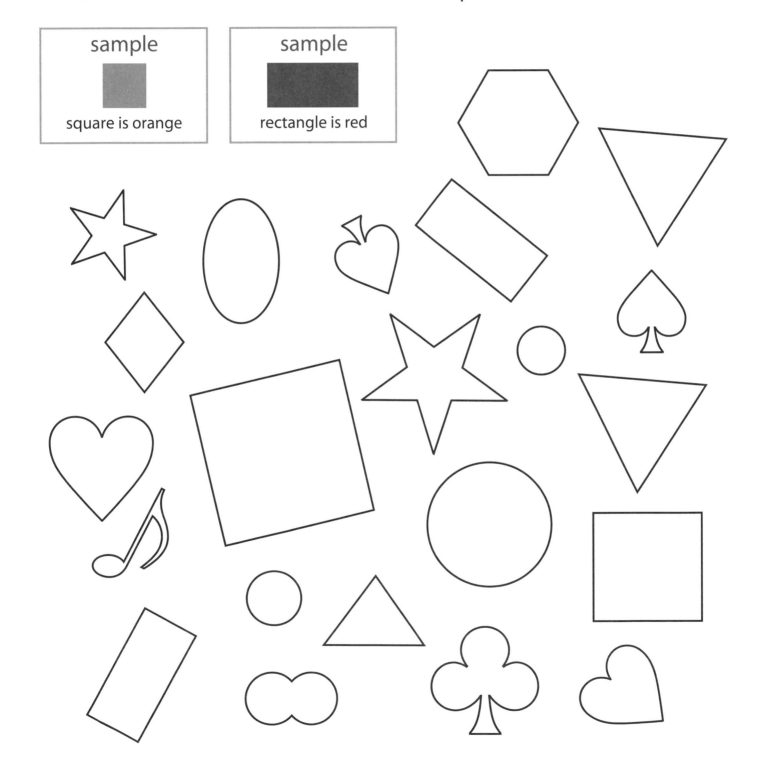

sample

square is orange

sample

rectangle is red

■ Find the shapes shown in the samples below.
  Then color them the same color as the sample.

sample	sample	sample
oval is green	triangle is purple	diamond is blue

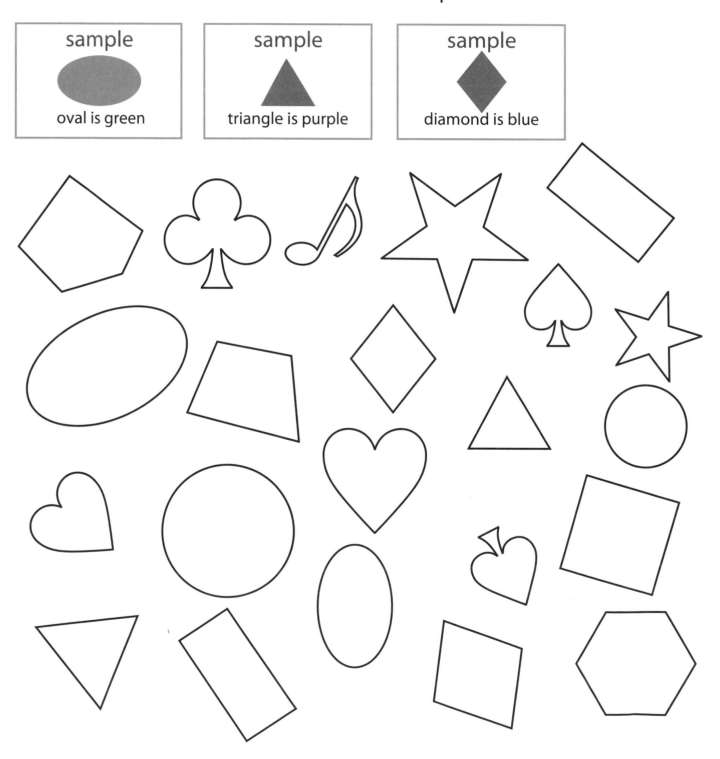

What is First?
What is Last?

Name

Date

To parents The following pages will help your child follow directions. Please give your child hints if he or she struggles to understand the questions.

■ Circle the first thing in each line below.

Front

Front

Front

■ Color the first thing in each line below.

Front

Front

Front

■ Circle the last thing in each line below.

Front

Front

Front

■ Color the last thing in each line below.

Front

Front

Front

58

Name

Date

To parents Now your child will review some of the concepts he or she has seen in this book. Remember that most of these topics are covered in kindergarten, and that the purpose of this book is to identify what particular skills your child may want to work on. Please see our line of preschool workbooks for further instruction.

■ Draw a line from 1 to 30 in order while saying each number aloud.

(elephant)

How many are there? Write the numbers.

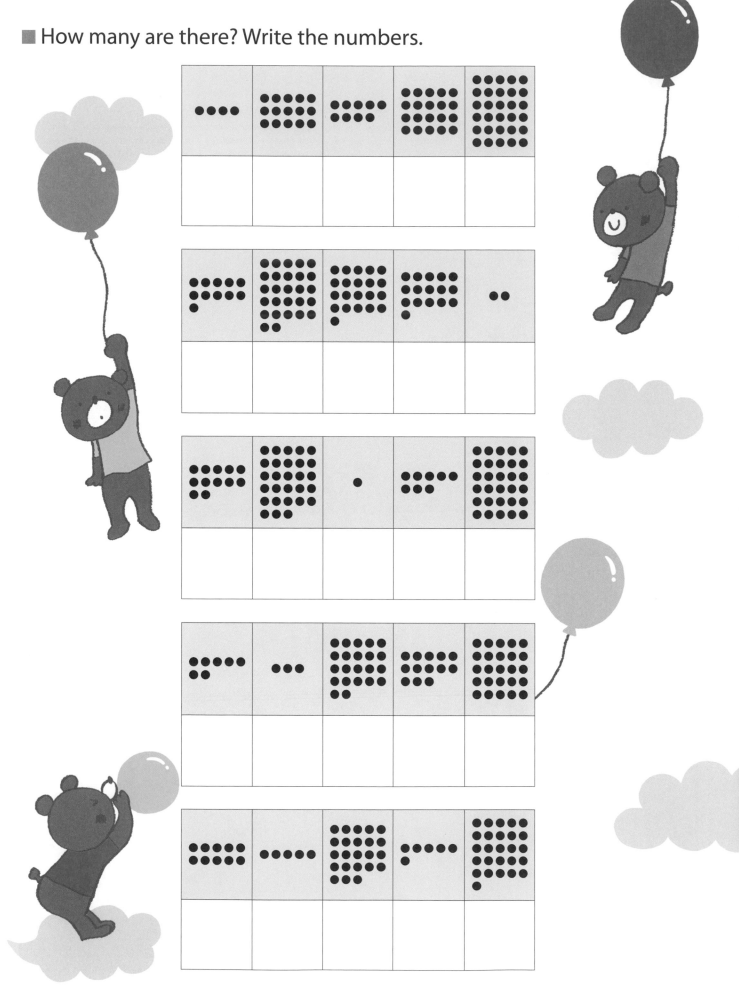

Review

Name

....

Date

To parents Remember to congratulate your child for all the work he or she has done. Your child will continue to work on these concepts in kindergarten. Keeping him or her interested and confident is a key part of creating a self-motivated learner!

■ Fill in the missing numbers. Say each number aloud.

1		3		5
6		8		10
11		13		15
16		18		20
21		23		25
26		28		30

1				
				15
				30

61

■ Find the shapes shown in the samples below.
  Then color them the same color as the sample.

sample	sample	sample	sample	sample
circle is green	square is orange	triangle is blue	rectangle is red	diamond is yellow

KUMON

Certificate of Achievement

is hereby congratulated on completing

Are You Ready for Kindergarten?   Math Skills

, 20

Presented on

Parent or Guardian